Table of Contents

Introduction

Thank you for downloading the book, *Kindle Publishing Guide – How to Create and Sell eBooks From Start to Finish* .

The book is meant to help you get started publishing books and generating money online with Amazon Kindle through the KDP program. This book is an A-Z book that shows everything in detail, with illustrations and images, each of them explained. The book contains 2 main parts: Part 1, how to create your book and Part 2, how to promote and sell your book.

By reading this book, you will learn:

- What Kindle Direct Publishing is
- The Benefits of Kindle Direct Publishing
- What you need to know to get started
- How to create a book from start to finish
- The tools Amazon offers
- How Amazon helps you market your book
- How to promote your book
- How to be productive
- How to create business from KDP

- How to generate thousands of dollars from KDP

PART 1: Publishing Your Book

Chapter 1: What is KDP?

Amazon is among the biggest marketplaces on the web that offers any kind of product – physical products, audio products, digital products, TV shows, music, movies, exclusive programs, etc. The huge potential Amazon has over other online platforms (such as eBay or Google) makes it the #1 leader in the worldwide e-commerce market.

KDP = Kindle Direct Publishing (or in other words, Kindle self-publishing) – It is a service offered exclusively by Amazon to people who want to publish their own books.

You will now think, "Well, I'm not a writer, this isn't for me." I thought so, too, at the very first beginning, but it's totally different. Anyone can write a book about any topic, it's simple and fast, you just put some words of your own, create pages, make up a good title, and upload the book. It will bring you money each month.

In the following chapters, I will show you how to create a book from start to finish to the point where it will make money for you. You have minimum investment for this type of business. If you have some knowledge about Adobe Photoshop or other photo editing software, you can even publish books with $0 investment.

Kindle Direct Publishing is now the fastest online platform that generates a fast return on your investments (books). The profit you can obtain by publishing Kindle eBooks is enormous; there are people on Amazon who make a fortune from selling eBooks.

Chapter 2: Setting Up Your Account and Preparing for Publishing

To get started as fast as possible, you need to create a KDP account, which is different from the Amazon account you have. That's right, if you already have an Amazon account you use to buy products online, you will need a different account to create and where you will upload your books.

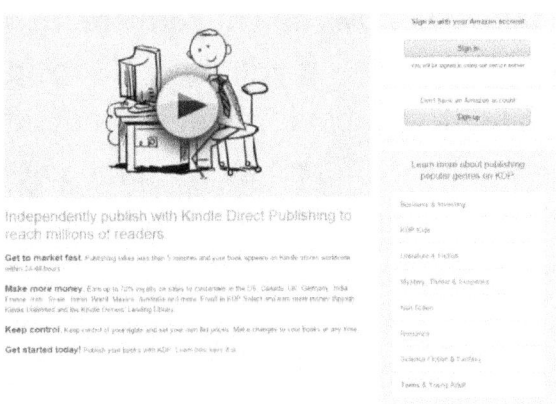

To create an account, you have to go to www.kdp.amazon.com and you will be asked a few things about yourself – Name, Address, Email, Credit Card (you will need this, otherwise, you can't set up an account).

When you set up your account, make sure to create the account depending on where you are publishing books from. For example, if you are from the US, you will need a $ (dollar) account, if you are from Europe, the account they require is in EURO and so on, every detail for every country is there.

Once you have completed all of these, you will need to complete TAX Information, which is very important. Without setting this, you will not be allowed to publish any books. You will have to complete data that will tell you how much you are to paying in Withholding Tax Rate – if you have US residency, you will pay 15%, if you have residency outside the US, you will pay 30%. Unfortunately, some countries are not eligible for using KDP, but maybe they will soon (the list is mentioned there). What's more interesting is that if you have residency in a country that has tax treaty with the US, you will also pay 15% but you will need to complete an EIN code or to give an ITIN number. Otherwise, you will pay 30% as well.

Tax Information

✓ Complete

Your tax information was received on 11/26/2014
*Applicable withholding rate 30% (What's this?)

Update Tax Information   Tax Interview Help Guide

Once you complete all of these fields, you can go to your dashboard and add new titles of your own. From there, in a matter of days, you will be capable of uploading and generating passive income.

Chapter 3: How Much Money Can You Make with Kindle Direct Publishing?

I honestly can't answer to this question because there is no exact answer. The potential is endless. You can make from $10 for a book up to a $1,000,000 or even more. Yes, actually, you can really generate $1,000,000 within a few months if you are a bestselling author. Let me give you a short example – if you are #1 in the whole Kindle paid store, you will sell at least 3,500 – 5,000 or even more copies a day. At this moment, the #1 book in Kindle store is a fiction book, it costs 4.99 including VAT and it has multiple formats – Audible, MP3 CD, Paperback, and Digital (Kindle) version, each of them priced differently.

For each purchase for Kindle, at $4.99, the author earns $2.83 (the actual price is $4.05 + VAT = $4.99 total price for the customer). Because the author has the book in the 70% royalty section (I will cover this in the next chapters), he earns $2.83/purchase. For 4,000 copies/day, the author earns 4,000 x $2.83 = $11,320 in one day and generally, when someone moves into the first place, it stays there from 2 weeks to even 3 months or so. Then it slowly moves to lower places, but even so, the author will sell 2,000–3,000 copies, but let's leave this behind for the moment and focus on how much money that author makes in 1 month in the 1st place in the Paid Kindle store:

$11,320 x 30 days = $339,600 for 1 book

So, the author makes all that cash in just 1 month. Imagine that the seller will go down in rank slowly and he will still make over $200,000 from selling Kindle eBooks. Now, I didn't mention that he makes a lot of money from the other formats, too, from Audible and Paperback formats he sells. He makes over $100,000 from that, too. All of these numbers are a minimum amount of what an author in 1st place is actually making. He can sell over 5,000, 6,000, or maybe 10,000 copies a day. And that's not all, the author makes another $100,000 - $200,000 a month from borrows (I will cover this next).

You are probably wondering to yourself, "How do I know from how many copies a bestselling author sells every day?" Well, there is nice tool for publishers to track their rank. It's called kdpcalculator, and to access it, go to

http://kdpcalculator.com

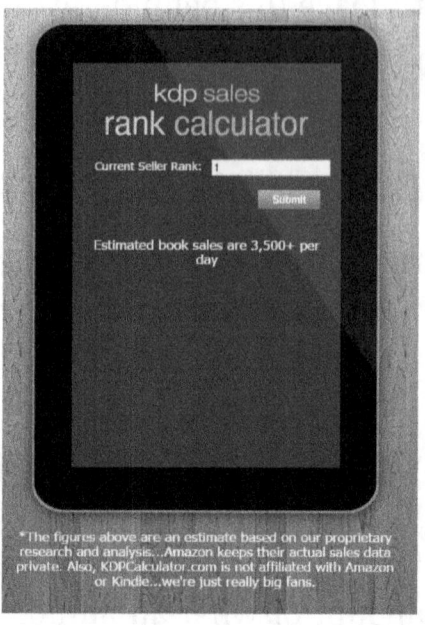

I just wanted to show you how powerful Amazon can be for bestselling authors. I know that you are starting for the very first time and you will not be able to make such a big amount of money if you aren't a real author and you are good at it. Those people who earn that amount of money are bestselling authors, they are novelists and they've wrote books their entire lives. This is not our case, so let's focus on what we need most.

If you publish an average book (30 – 50 pages) on a topic of your own (for example, Paleo Diet), you will make on average, around $50-$100 for a book. When you publish books and you will have a big number of books, you will have niches that will bring you as little as $20, others $200-$300, and others even $500–$1000/ month. It all depends on the market you pick, the niche of the book and on how good the book is: how many reviews it has, how good the cover looks, what title it has, etc. There are a lot of factors that influence your sales and we will discuss them all in the following chapters.

Let's take a real example, one of my books. I will show you exactly how much money I make with one book (I will keep the name of the book private).

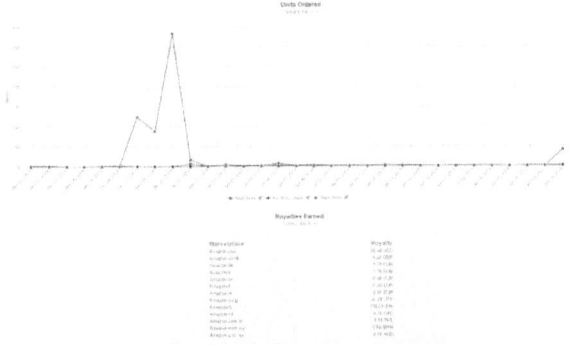

This graphs will appear in your dashboard. It shows you how many units you have (free units, borrowed units – KOLL/KU and paid units).

I was able to generate $58.44 from the US store, 5.28GBP from the UK store, and the other markets where my book has been sold – Germany, France, Japan, India, and Canada. All of these currencies will be automatically converted in the currency in which you will get your money (Euro, USD, etc.)

So, in total, I have made $77.17 only from paid units during 1 month. The graph has that green line that represents the free units. Let me take that off so you can see my sales. I also had 12 borrows for the past 30 days for that book and I will find out at the end of the month how much borrows were paid (if the person who borrows your book doesn't read at least 10% of the book, you will not be paid). You will find that out separately from the royalty section from above. You will find this information in the "Prior Month Royalties" section each month on 15th. So from the borrows and the royalties I have earned, I have made a total of $93.97 for that book, which is priced at $2.99 and has 35 pages.

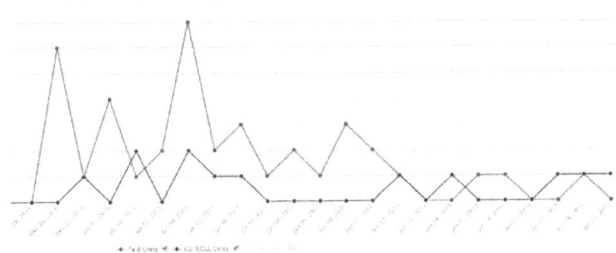

The red line represents the paid units and the blue line represents the number of borrows that I have received.

People can borrow your book for free (it's not actually free, you pay $9.99/month or you get it free if you have signed up for the prime membership, which is $99/year), any books that are enrolled in the KDP Select program (I will cover that next).

For you as an author, you get an amount of money at the end of each month, depending on how many books were borrowed that month on the whole Kindle store.

There is a Global Fund for KDP Select each month, the amount for January is $3 Million. The amount is collected from the Kindle Unlimited (KU) subscriptions and from Prime membership subscriptions and that Global Fund is divided to the total number of borrows for that month. In other words, you will get, in average, between $1.5 and $2 for 1 borrow, which is very good.

Chapter 4: Market Research

Which niche you choose to write about is one of the most important aspects of the book. The niche you pick has to pass a few steps to become a profitable one:

1. It shouldn't be too broad or too narrow at the same time
2. Look to see if there is market for that niche
3. Look for your niche from categories to subcategories and micro-categories

I will show you how to do this step by step and give you examples so you can understand the whole process.

1. Let's pick a random niche, let's take, for example "Leadership" as a niche and as a keyword. If you simply type "Leadership" in Amazon's search bar, you will get a large number of results, so it's too broad and you will not be able to outrank all of those books, even with the best book in the world.

A number of results of 27,481 is insanely big and it's impossible for you to make your book show up in the first searches. The books that you see up are old, have good reviews, they're being bought daily, and the author is probably also popular.

Now, if you type in the search bar "Leadership Coaching for beginners", you will get 3 results, so it isn't good either.

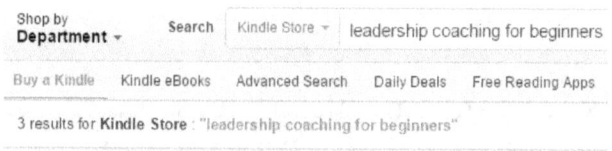

So, the key is to find a keyword/title for which you have an average number of results, to be between narrow and broad – not too narrow, but not too broad at the same time. A number of 300–1,000 results is a good choice for a title/niche/keyword for your book.

If we type "Leadership Coaching", you will get 1,085 results, which is okay. This number isn't impossible to outrank. After you do a free promotion (I will explain this in the next chapters) and get a large number of downloads, you will outrank most of the books and you will be in the first 1-6 books that show up.

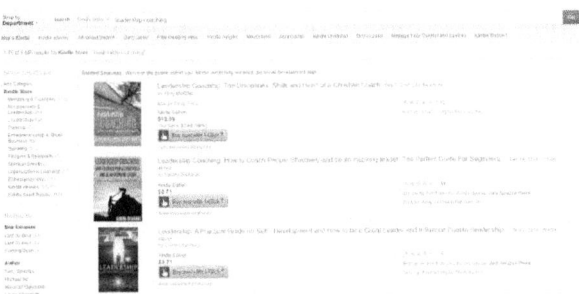

TIP: This algorithm is available for choosing the right keywords as well, not too narrow, not too broad, it's simple to remember.

2. Check if there is any market

If you decided you would like to write about "Leadership Coaching" here's what you need to do:

- Search for "Leadership Coaching" or the title/niche you want to write about
- Click on the first 6 books that show up and track the sales ranking like in the following picture

and use the KDP calculator (I mentioned in the previous chapter)

Amazon Best Sellers Rank: #60,328 Paid in Kindle Store (See Top 100 Paid in Kindle Store)
#25 in Kindle Store > Kindle eBooks > Business & Money > Business Life > Mentoring & Coaching
#63 in Books > Business & Money > Management & Leadership > Mentoring & Coaching
#69 in Kindle Store > Kindle Short Reads > One hour (33-43 pages) > Business & Money

The book with these rankings is actually a good book. It won't bring you thousands of dollars but it will bring you a couple of hundred dollars per month, passively.

#60,328 Paid in Kindle Store means that your book will sell 2-3 copies a day. If you price the book at $2.99, for example, you will earn $2.09/download and for 3 copies a day, you will earn a total of $6.27/day. It doesn't sound much, but in a month, you will get $188.1 for that book with that ranking. Sounds good, doesn't it?

- Check when was the book published – books that are recently published are automatically boosted by Amazon to get additional sales and if a book is older than 3 months and still sells well, it means that it's a good and profitable niche for a longer period of time. You don't want to write a book and to lose sales within 2 months, do you?
- See how much competition you have for that niche. If there are too many books on the same

niche, even if it's a good market for it, you won't get too many sales because there will be other authors with older and better books than yours (at the beginning) and you won't earn too much.

The thing is that it must be a good balance between these aspects and keep in mind that every niche has its own market, its own competition. You will have books that sell better than others because of these factors plus one more – luck. If you are lucky enough, sometimes, it's enough to make good sales.

3. When you want to make sure that your niche is a good one, go from the main category to subcategories and to the lowest and smallest micro-category (the narrowest). By doing this, you will see which is narrow and which is not and you will see some titles that sell really well and some titles that sell really bad – study (do market research) for 10 books or even more and choose what fits you best.

So follow the images from left to right: Firstly, click on "Kindle Best Sellers" so you can see the top 100 paid and 100 free in that category. Next, you go to "Business Life", it's a general Category. Next, you go to "Management & Leadership" and then, "Leadership", the last micro-category. You will see there what you are interested in: the top paid 100 books in Leadership. From there, see what sells best and it will be easier for you to pick your final title and niche to write about.

Tip: When you upload your book on KDP, there you will be different, but similar categories and subcategories.

Chapter 5: How to Choose a Good Title for Your Book

As soon as you go through the previous chapters and find a good niche, you will need to find a good title and some good keywords (these should be based on what content you have in your book). I will now show you some examples of good titles and bad titles.

A good title should have:

1. At least one benefit. You can put more as well, but people want to know what value they will get from your book.
2. Include "know-hows" and "how to dos" in your title.
3. Make sure that your title contains keywords (research for the best ones, remember from the previous chapters – not too narrow, not too broad).

Examples: *How to Start a Business from Home – 10 Proven Online Income Streams that Will Give You Financial Freedom: The Ultimate Guide for Beginners*

This is the title from my other book, which describes 10 income streams (one of them is Kindle Publishing, this is the second book from that series). The title has a "how to" – How to start a business from home (it's also a good keyword for which you get 285 results if you type it). You also have benefits – you will learn 10 proven online income streams (that's one) and you will achieve financial freedom (that's the second benefit).

The title is long, it's descriptive, and it has keywords. For some of the keywords, your book (in this case, my book) will appear in the top of the list.

You can see the 285 results for the keyword you can find in the book's title.

Tips:

1. You should include your book as a part of a series (you will be asked somewhere – "Is this book a part of a series?" – You should say yes, even if it isn't. You should make a series because your books promote each other. When

someone clicks on the series title, all of your books from that series can be seen easily.

2. Include as many keywords as you can: in the description, title, subtitle, series title, the keywords field when you upload the book (up to 7 keywords, I will cover this in the following chapters).

Bad Titles

How you can see if a title is good or not:

1. The title is short.
2. It has no benefits.
3. It doesn't tell you anything about the book.

Examples: *How to Start a Business: Starting a Business*

(Look in the last image, the third book has a BAD TITLE)

Tip: The KEYWORDS are everything for every book.

Chapter 6: How to Write and Format Your Book

As soon as you finish finding a good niche (not too narrow, not too broad), go in Microsoft Word if you are using Windows or Pages if you are using Mac OS.

Organize your book in chapters, describe everything clearly and write as much as you want.

Make sure to make an introduction, chapters, and a conclusion.

Create a Table of Contents with Bookmarks and Hyperlinks.

Tips:

1. Don't make grammar mistakes, people (readers) hate when they see mistakes in a book even though it's nearly impossible to see a book with absolutely zero mistakes.
2. Don't make your books too short, people will think that you are selling an article, not a book. Make books with at least 30 pages and choose your price (I will cover this in the following chapters).

How to Create Bookmarks in Microsoft Word (Sorry, I don't have Mac OS for those who wanted)

As soon as you write the table of contents at the beginning and you finished your book, you will have to create bookmarks. You simply select each chapter and click on "Insert" and then "Bookmark".

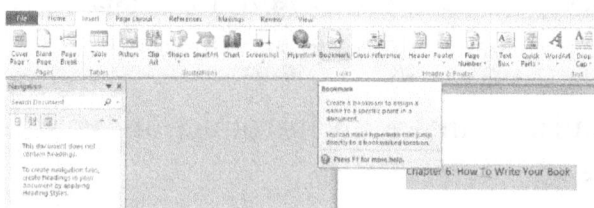

Create all the bookmarks for every chapter, for the Table of Contents as well and for the Introduction and Conclusion as well (take my book as an example) and then Insert the Hyperlinks on each of them (they will appear blue and underlined).

Click on Insert => Hyperlink => and click on Bookmarks, choose the corresponding bookmark with the hyperlink that you want to use.

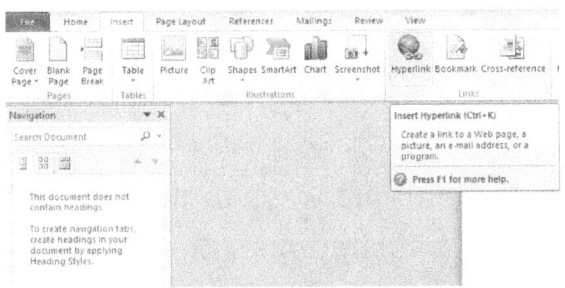

If you don't want to write your book and you hire someone else to write your books, make sure to proofread your book and to format it correctly. You should also create the table of contents and the chapters with bookmarks and hyperlinks.

The reason you should do all of these is to make it easier for your readers to go through the chapters. If you had 200 pages, you wouldn't want to slide between pages 200 times if you want to read a passage or a chapter from that book.

Tip: Kindle format won't recognize your Table of Contents if you don't write a TOC bookmark for the Table of Contents. Kindle looks for TOC when you put hyperlinks and so, make sure not to forget this aspect.

Chapter 7: How to Make Your Cover

There are multiple ways to design your cover, but you have 4 main options:

1. You design the cover yourself in a photo editing software like Adobe Photoshop.
2. You make a simple cover using Kindle Cover Creator – when you finish your book, you go to your KDP account, you complete the required fields and when it requires your cover, click on "Launch Cover Creator" and it will guide you step by step on how to create your own cover (image, title, author, etc.).

3. If you want a cover to look a little bit better than using cover creator and you want to sit more comfortable, go on www.Fiverr.com and

request a cover design. It will only cost you $5 and you will have it ready between 12 hours and 4 days, depending on what you request.

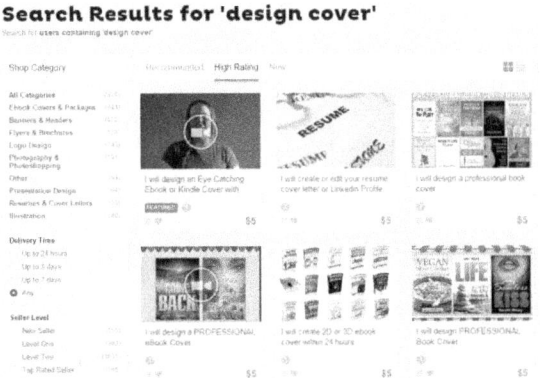

4. If you want a premium and unique design, you go to www.99designs.com and you will pay from $299 to $1,199 for a premium cover. You will get different high quality designs (from 25 to 35 designs) and you will be able to choose from them. Choose only what you like (by rating them). All of those designers will enter a contest (your project, your cover) and they will compete between themselves for the best design. That's why it's so expensive, but it is sometimes worth it if you make a book that represents you or you just want a premium quality.

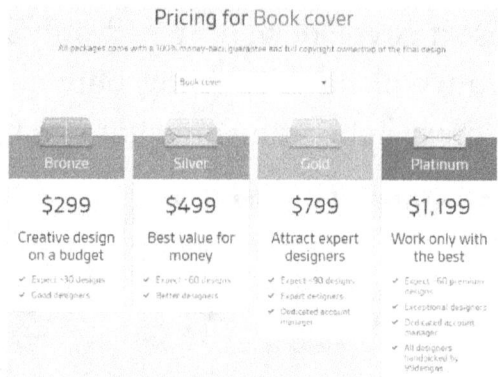

Pricing for Book cover

All packages come with a 100% money-back guarantee and full copyright ownership of the final design

	Bronze	Silver	Gold	Platinum
	$299	**$499**	**$799**	**$1,199**
	Creative design on a budget	Best value for money	Attract expert designers	Work only with the best
	✓ Expect ~30 designs	✓ Expect ~60 designs	✓ Expect ~90 designs	✓ Expect ~60 premium designs
	✓ Good designers	✓ Better designers	✓ Expert designers	✓ Exceptional designers
			✓ Dedicated account manager	✓ Dedicated account manager
				✓ All designers handpicked by 99designs

To be honest, I like to sit comfortable and use the services offered by Fiverr, so I order my covers there and relax until they are done. $5 or $10 and you are done. Nice and clean. I advise you to do the same for your upcoming books.

Tip: If you want to use Cover Creator, you will create your cover in a few minutes when you upload the book – photo in the next chapter.

Chapter 8: Uploading Your Book on Kindle

Congratulations! You have finished your book, you have written your book, and you have designed/ordered a cover for your book, now you have to upload your book on Kindle to make money.

First of all, you go to your KDP account on www.kdp.amazon.com and you go to "Bookshelf". Then you click on "Add new title" above in the left corner.

The first thing that you will see after you click on "Add new title" will be "Introducing KDP Select", so click on the box to enroll in KDP Select; it offers a lot of good promotional tools plus Kindle Unlimited (for borrowing your books). I strongly advise you to enroll in this program and not to ignore it. It can boost your sales by over 600%, so it's very important.

Then, you enter your title and subtitle. The title is mandatory, and the subtitle is optional but I strongly recommend you make up good subtitle as well (include keywords, as many keywords as you can – look to the previous chapters).

Then you will be asked, "Is this book a part of a series?" – click on yes even if it isn't and put more keywords or a real series for your book (or books).

You will be asked to write a description (up to 4,000 words) next. Write as much as you possibly can – describe your book, what readers will find in it, what benefits the book will bring to the readers, put some good quotes (optional) and tell people the best about your book, and invite them to check it out for themselves. This is very important for your future sales.

Next, you will have to put the contributors (author, editor, etc.) – you will only have to put the author in most of the cases if you are a Self-Publisher. I advise you to use Pen Names (I will cover this in the following chapters), but if you want to, you can use your real name as well.

Select the language that you want to write your book (most of the authors write their books in English). Then select "This is not a public domain work" – this is very important.

Then you are asked to choose your categories – make sure to choose the best categories that fit your book into. You can choose 2 categories; these will help rank your book higher or even make you a bestseller so choose them wisely.

Then here's come the magic I was speaking about in the previous chapters: choosing your keywords – up to 7 keywords. So what exactly is a keyword and why are they so important? A keyword is not just a word, it's a small sentence people are searching for. "How to write a book" – that's a keyword; "Leadership Coaching For Beginners" – I hope you've got the idea. That's what you have to choose here, in this section, the keywords (use all of the 7 keywords you are allowed to – the more keywords, the more readers you reach, the more money you make).

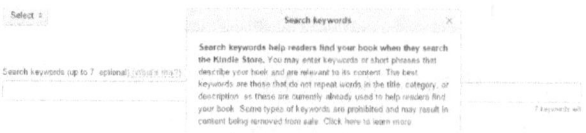

Next, you will be asked if you want to release your book now or if you want to create a pre-order. Pre-orders help your book increase in sales and they create emotion and that feeling that you don't have any more patience for a product to be released (for popular authors or so, I think it works great). I honestly haven't used this before, but you can use it if you want to after you have a number of books already released.

As soon as you finish all of these, you will be asked next to upload your cover, the one you ordered on Fiverr, 99designs, or the one you designed yourself. However, as I said earlier, you can create a 100% free cover using Cover Creator.

5. Upload or Create a Book Cover

Upload an existing cover, or design a high-quality cover with Cover Creator. (optional)

No Cover Available

I have a book cover designed and ready to upload
Please read our Cover guidelines

Browse for image...

I want to design a cover using the Cover Creator (beta).

Launch Cover Creator

Then you will be asked to upload your content (your .doc file for word or your file from Mac OS). Upload it there and it will be automatically converted into the Kindle format. It will take a while to upload – less than 1 minute for short books without images or up to 10 minutes or so. It depends on how large the book is and how many images the book has. Be aware that Amazon has a "digital delivery price" – they charge you about \$0.14/MB to deliver wirelessly so try to maintain a good ratio for every book you release.

After you upload your content, Amazon will tell you if you have any spelling mistakes and it will even show you where those are. You should have zero spelling mistakes when you upload your book.

You can preview your book to see how it looks on every device – on Kindle Fire HDX 7 inch/8.9

inch/iPad, etc. You will know if the view is okay and if there are any errors there. It's a useful tool.

Once you finish completing all of these fields, you can click on "Save and continue" and you will be guided to a new set of fields to complete – pricing and rights.

You can choose to sell your book on individual territories or worldwide (I always choose worldwide).

You are asked about pricing. This is important – you can choose between 2 types of royalties – 35% or 70%. You will get 35% royalties for books priced anywhere from $0 to $200 except the range $2.99 – $9.99 and you will get 70% royalty if you price the book between $2.99 and $9.99 so try to make the books in such a manner that you can price them at $2.99 or $3.99 or up to $9.99.

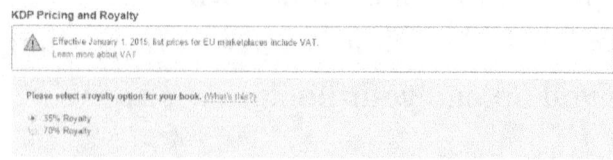

You will see a table with all the conversions in other currencies and you will also see how much you earn for each sale. For example, if you choose to sell your book for $0.99, you will get $0.35 royalty. However, if you choose 70% royalty and price your book for $2.99, you will get $2.09.

Tip: Don't forget about the delivery costs – Amazon charges you about $0.12/MB for transferring eBooks wirelessly, so the bigger the book and the more pictures you put in the book, the less you earn.

Soon after you finish choosing your royalty option, you will be asked if you want to enroll your book in the "Matchbook Program" – if you agree to this, a customer who buys the paperback version of your book will get the kindle edition for free. If you want to release a paperback version, I advise you to enroll in this program as well.

Then, you will be asked if you want to lend your book. Click on "Allow lending"; you will get, on average, $1.5/borrow. If are you already enrolled in KDP Select, it means that you agreed with Kindle Unlimited, which is a borrowing service as well. Here, where you are asked to allow the book for lending, is another service, Kindle Online Lending Library (KOLL). So allow lending.

10. Kindle MatchBook

☐ Enroll this book in the Kindle MatchBook program. (Details)

11. Kindle Book Lending

☑ Allow lending for this book (Details)

Kindle Book Lending	×
Enrollment in Kindle Book Lending will allow users to lend your book after purchasing to their friends and family for a duration of 14 days. For full details, review the Kindle Book Lending Program.	

And you are almost done! Click on save and publish and Amazon will publish your book live between 12 and 48 hours (usually 12 hours for English books). Click on "Save and Publish" and you are DONE.

Chapter 9: How Do You Get Paid?

Royalties

Royalties are the commission that you receive from selling any products (in our case, eBooks) and it depends on the product's price. As I showed earlier, there are two main types of royalties – the 35% and the 70% royalty.

It's tricky at the beginning, as most authors want as much profit as possible and they go straight to $2.99 or $3.99 or even more to get the maximum royalty (70%). The thing is that when you publish your book for the first time, it has no reviews, it can be found nowhere on Amazon, you are outranked by almost all the book in same category, and if you have a bigger price ($2.99), you won't get any sales.

At first, put your book at $0.99 and let the downloads come easily so you can get some reviews and rank higher at the same time. As soon as you reach at least 5 reviews, then you should put your book for $2.99 (and make sure to have a decent number of pages, no one likes $2.99 books with 15 pages).

When does Amazon pay you?

Amazon generates a report each month on 15th, which tells you how much money you made for the previous month. You will see the money in your bank account between 25th and 28th day of the month (and the money you receive is from the previous month).

Tip: The royalties you see in the dashboard are only from paid units (sales) – in the report, you will have a larger amount of money as you are paid for borrows, too. You can see the monthly report on every 15th day of the month in the section "Prior Months' Royalties".

So you get paid every 30 days, usually on 28th each month. If you have just started, you will see your first paycheck after 60 days – you get paid for 2 months and then month after month. They have this policy as most of the authors don't make too many sales in their first month and they grow in the second month.

Tip: Sales tend to fluctuate all the time. If you have 10 books (average quality books), it's possible to see 20 sales in one day, while on some days, you will have zero sales or so. It fluctuates all the time, so don't panic if you have such bad days. Every author on Amazon has them.

Sales fluctuate every month – in January, people don't have too much money, so it's a weak month for sales; in December, cookbooks sell well as Christmas knocks at the door and a lot of people want to learn how to cook or they want to try new recipes. There are books that sell all the time, but this isn't a rule. Take the sales fluctuations into consideration, it's normal to be that way.

Part 2: Promoting Your Book

Chapter 1: The Importance of Promoting Your Book

Promoting a product is sometimes even more important than the product itself. If you have an excellent 5 star product that anyone would definitely like that isn't promoted properly, then you might not get the results that you're expecting. However, if you have an average quality product that isn't impressive, if it's promoted or even over promoted, you will get tons of sales and an increased profit.

The same story is here. No matter how good your eBook will be, you won't see any profit until you promote it and in this part of the book, I will show you exactly how to promote your book and where to promote your book.

There are a lot of methods that are really efficient for promoting books on Kindle; you may know few of them, but I'm convinced you will find a lot of new things.

Chapter 2: KDP Promotional Tools

As you may have noticed, when you publish your book on Kindle, you are asked if you want to enroll in KDP Select. This is the most powerful promotional tool that you are going to use, and you are going to maximize the potential of this powerful tool with what I am about to show you next.

Before we go on to that, let me first show you what tools KDP Select offers and how they can be used.

First of all, KDP Select offers two main different tools: Free Promo Days and Countdown Deals.

1. Free Promo Days – you are allowed to promote your eBook for free for 5 days every 90 days. That means that your book will be $0.00 for a limited time in which users will grab your book. It won't sound too fancy for you, because you have probably worked hard to finish that book, or you may have paid money for it to be written and others can have it for free.

Even if it doesn't sound nice, this really helps you to sell your book. It increases the potential to sell your book by up to 600%! You will wonder how, and I did the same in the beginning. The answer is – you choose a number of keywords (7 keywords + title + subtitle – see previous chapters) and when people are downloading your book, those units are for Amazon "paid units" but they are at $0.00. So your book will rank higher in Amazon's searches, people will start finding you easily, you will be seen faster, and Amazon will recommend your book to others who downloaded/purchased books from a similar category.

The question is, how many downloads do you need during the promo to outrank more than 80% of the books from your category?

The answer is a lot, as many as possible. To get as many downloads as possible, there are some tricks and some things to do while your book is on the free limited period. We'll discuss this in the following chapters.

2. Countdown Deals - if you have a big book or you already have a paperback version and you really don't want to give your book away for free, you can use countdown deals – the price of the book will start at a given price (for example $0.99) and it will raise day by day with $1.00 or so until it reaches the original price.

Amazon has a separate category for Countdown Deals, and a lot of people are actually looking for this kind of limited time offer deals.

Tip – you can choose only one from the 2 types of promotion – either Free Promotional Days or Countdown Deals. I honestly always choose Free Promotional Days and what I am about to share with you next is based on Free Promotional Days.

Important!

1. If you sign up for "KDP Select", you have to sell your books exclusively on Amazon and nowhere else (there are a lot of places where you can sell your book – Smashwords, Barnes & Noble, etc.)
2. You can use the promotional days for 5 days every 90 days (sorry for the repetition), so use them wisely.

Chapter 3: How to Set Up a Promotion

This is the easiest part of what awaits you next.

As soon as your book is published and enrolled in KDP, you go to your Bookshelf and click on "Manage Benefits" below the KDP Select column.

Then you will have to choose between Countdown Deals and Free Promo Days – set your promotion when you want. I usually like to go for 2 days or 3 days at once, it's not a good option to use all of your days at once, as most of the readers already downloaded your book and you will have less downloads in the last 1-2 days of free promo.

Run a price promotion for your book on Amazon

Create a new promotion

Sign your book up for one of the following promotional programs

Only one promotional program can be enabled per enrollment period. Please select either Kindle Countdown Deals or Free Book Promotion

| Kindle Countdown Deal | ⚠ This book is currently ineligible for a Free Book Deal (Why?) |
| Free Book Promotion | |

It says there that my book is ineligible for a Free Book Deal as I have already used my 5 days. I will be able to run Free Book Deals 90 days after I published the book.

Chapter 4: Promoting Your Book on Free Websites

There are a lot of websites where a lot of passionate readers subscribe for good reads, free reads, books on different categories, etc. The idea is that if you have a free book, let people know that you have a freebie a few days before the promotion starts so they will already know.

By putting your free book on websites, the number of downloads will increase significantly for each website you use. The more you use, the better it is.

Where can you put your book for free?

There arc actually lots of websites, I know only few of them, but they have seemed to be helpful for me. Be aware that some websites will charge you if you want your book to be promoted more on that website, but most of the websites are free.

Here's a short list of 10 websites I usually like to use:

www.pixelofink.com

www.bargainbookhunter.com

www.thatbookplace.com

www.ebookshabit.com

www.freebookshub.com

www.ebooklister.com

www.ebooksfreedaily.com

www.frugalfreebies.com

www.onehundredfreebooks.com

www.snicklist.com

Use all of these websites and you will increase your number of downloads a lot. Remember, a big number of downloads will rank you higher and will increase your chances of selling books over 600%.

Tip: If you don't have time, you can use the services from www.fiverr.com for $5. There are some gigs there that submit your book to 10 websites for $5-$20 websites for $10 or $15 and so on, up to $40 for 40-50 websites as I remember.

Check out my Gig Extras

Basic Gig Quantity   `1 ($5)` ▾

Submit your free promotion to a total of 20 sites and send you
my popular PDF, Taming Amazon
(+2 days)   `1 ($10)` ▾

Submit your free promotion to a total of 30 sites and send you
my popular PDF, Taming Amazon
(+2 days)   `1 ($20)` ▾

Submit to a total of 40 sites, send you my PDF, and feature on
my website, NewFreeKindleBooks.com
(+2 days)   `1 ($40)` ▾

Give you my list of over 50 links to the forms on each site so
you can fill out your book's details
(+2 days)   `1 ($10)` ▾

Order Now ($5)

Chapter 5: Promoting Your Book on Facebook

Facebook is also a really powerful tool for promoting different products. Here, you have multiple possibilities for how to promote your book and I will discuss each one of them.

1. Promote by creating a Fan Page for your book.
2. Pay for Facebook Advertising.
3. Share with your friends/circles.
4. Join groups for different niches and share your book there.
5. Pay for someone else to share your book in multiple groups.
6. Use Hash Tags

1. To attract more potential readers and customers, and to sell more copies of your book, a Fan Page on Facebook can be the perfect solution – you can reach millions (readers) if you have an outstanding book. If you have invested a lot in creating a book, you have worked a lot and put a lot of value in writing a

masterpiece, creating a Fan Page is a must for you as an author.

It works nice for any kind of book, especially if you promote that Fan Page even further – give away the book for free, sign up on different websites and make your Fan Page popular. The more popular it becomes, the more likes you will have and so... the more customers you will have for that book.

2. Pay for ads on Facebook (Facebook Advertising). It's cheap and efficient – a lot of people will see ads with your books on their profile, and if they are interested, they will click on your book and buy it. You will pay from $5 to $20 for a limited time and Facebook will provide you a minimum number of likes (for Fan Pages for example) – remember the previous step, the more likes you get, the more readers you reach.

3. Share your book on your profile page. Your friends will see what you have shared. If you do not have too many "friends", create a business account for Facebook and add as many as possible, up to 5000 Friends for a personal account. Imagine that if you share your book to 5,000 people, at least 1,000 will click to see what the book is about, and from that 1,000, at least 100 will eventually buy your book.

4. Join Groups on Facebook on different topics. For example, if you have a cookbook and you want to promote your book while it's free (Free Promo – KDP Select). Share your book wherever you can; a bigger number of free downloads will boost your sales after the promotion. If you have a cookbook about Paleo, search for "Paleo" closed groups and share your book there. There are groups from 1,000 people to more than 1,000,000 and you will surely boost your download rate during the free promo.

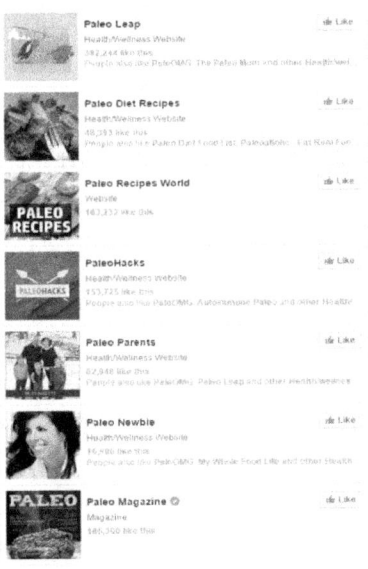

5. Pay someone else to promote your book on Facebook – go to www.Fiverr.com and pay gigs to promote your book starting with $5 and up to $40. They will share your book on their Fan Pages, private profiles, closed groups, or even secret groups you do not have access to. They will provide you a proof sheet in which you will see exactly where they have promoted your book.

   After all, $5-$10 for a good promotion on Facebook is a real bargain for everyone.

6. Use Hash Tags when you post something on any website – use hash tags like: #freekindle, #freeebook, #kindle, #KDP, #freebook,

#amazon, #goodreads, #freereads, #freestuff etc.

In other words, Facebook is a really powerful tool for promoting any kind of product, especially digital ones, like your eBooks – putting them one click away for a person to buy your eBook on Amazon.

Chapter 6: Promote Your Book Using Social Media

Along with Facebook, which, in my opinion, is the most powerful social tool you can use, there are others, too, that can also boost your sales and downloads for your book. Here's a list of social media places where you can create accounts and promote your book (you can pay someone else to do this, too – Fiverr)

1. Twitter
2. Instagram
3. Pinterest
4. LinkedIn
5. Google+

These are the most common places where you can promote your book. A single account on these platforms will help you to succeed even more in promoting your book properly and to generate additional sales and downloads.

If you do not have any accounts on the platforms mentioned above, create an account for each of them and get started immediately – every person who sees your book can be a potential customer and you can reach customers worldwide.

Chapter 7: Free and Paid Advertising for Kindle Books

If you want to get the best results with your books on Kindle (or any other platform), you will need to invest in advertising.

Without any advertising or additional efforts to promote your book, you will probably see between 50 and 300 downloads in 24 hours – it generally depends on how many people will go on Kindle that day.

To see money coming in, you need to get over 2,000 downloads for a book (and even then, the success for that book is not guaranteed) and you can easily get them by paying for some services that will expose your work to a lot of readers.

Where can you promote your book?

Bookbub – the best service for books that you can find online – you pay from $40 to $2,000 depending on the niche and category, if it's free, if it's $0.99, or more. Generally, the biggest numbers come from this website – I've seen authors who received over 40,000 downloads using this service.

Freebooksy – you pay $50 -$100 and you should expect around 1,000–3,000 downloads depending on the niche. A good fiction book can get even more.

DigitalBookToday – pay between $15 and $100 and get hundreds or even thousands of downloads.

Fiverr – pay a gig to promote your book on 10–20 websites and get a few hundreds of downloads for $5 or $10.

eBookshabit – pay $10 for a guaranteed placement and get up to 1,000 downloads in 3-4 days. You can also pay for tweets on the same website.

BookSends – pay between $50 and $125 and you will see 500–3000 downloads for your book.

BuckBooks (free service for excellent books) – submit your book here if it has over 40 pages on Kindle and it's good quality (it has reviews, it's professionally formatted, it has a clean and catchy cover, and it doesn't have mistakes) and you will get 50–200 purchases at $0.99 and you will increase your paid rank in the Kindle Store – you will get more visibility in most of the categories. If the book is good, it will stay there; if not, it will drop fast.

BargainBooksy – pay $40 and you will get around 40-50 purchases at $0.99 to increase your ranking,

The idea is that you should pick 4-5 services ($150-$200 for) for the free promotion and at least 1 service for the paid promo at $0.99 – you will get 5,000–10,000 downloads and at least 100 purchases.

I had a book in which I invested $60 to launch it and $50 for the paid promo and the results were like this – I invested $110 in advertising, $40 in proofreading and editing, $20 in a professional cover, and in return, I received $700 in 2 months (the book had 110 pages and was nonfiction).

It's totally worth it.

Chapter 8: Reviews

Reviews for every book are crucial. I think everyone who is seeking for new reads on Amazon are willing to buy your books if the book has good reviews; it's the first thing that a customer is looking at. There are a lot of things that catches your eye when you are surfing on Amazon, but the reviews are the most important.

Personally, I don't buy a book if it doesn't have at least 50 pages and 10-15 reviews. That's just my personal way for selecting a good to very good book; others probably don't have this in mind, while others probably look at books that have 100 pages and over 30 reviews. It depends on how the customer sees the book.

The only thing that matters is that the more pages and the more reviews you get for a book, the higher the probability of selling that book.

Now, the big question – How do you get those reviews?

You have 4 possibilities:

1. Wait to naturally get those reviews. This is the best way for you so you don't get in any trouble with Amazon. This will take longer though if you are not a popular author.
2. Ask your friends/family to buy your book and leave a review. Even if most of the people do this, Amazon doesn't like this and if they see this, they will delete your review.
3. Exchange reviews with other authors. Again, Amazon doesn't like this at all and they delete both reviews from both authors if they see this.
4. Pay for reviews – on Freelancer, Fiver, etc.

What do I advise you to do? Use all the methods, *but* do not abuse them. A book, to start selling slowly, needs 4-5 positive reviews that you can get from the list above. I am not saying to buy tons of reviews, or to ask dozens of people to do that, just make sure you have a few reviews so you can start up your sales.

You won't get any sales until you have at least 2-3 reviews, or if you do, maybe someone bought it by mistake.

The most unfortunate thing on Amazon and on any other online store is that people don't bother at all to leave a review for what they have bought, unless:

1. The product is really *good* – outstanding, you have exalted your customer and you get a positive review.
2. The product is really *awful* – you really pissed off your customer and he leaves you a bad review.

Less than 2% of your customers will give you reviews, so it's important to get some reviews somehow. I'm serious, DO NOT ABUSE reviews from other people because you can get flagged, your reviews will be deleted, or you can even have your account suspended.

Tip: If your book is really awful for real and you will get several 1 star reviews, your book can be deleted (Amazon has this right).

So keep in mind – get a few reviews, but DO NOT ABUSE it; it's very important for your future Kindle business.

Chapter 9: Use Pen Names

Pen names are fiction names that everyone uses on Amazon for their books. There are few people who use their real name (popular authors, popular writers, or popular business people), but most of authors have pen names.

Why is it recommended to use pen names?

1. Different Niches/Categories – it's very important to have a pen name for one niche and I will tell you why. As an example, if you write only about business and then you publish health books, then about engineering, and then about medicine... How would it be? How would you be seen? The general author? It's ridiculous. If you want to write about different topics, use different pen names.
2. You become an "Expert" for a certain niche – if people will like a book of yours on that topic, they will certainly buy the others you sell, too.
3. If you have an awful book and you realize that, by changing your pen name and publishing other books, you will be unknown by those people. Imagine if you have 10 really good

books and you have a book that is horrible. People who buy that horrible book will ignore all the other 10 books you have for sale.

4. You maintain a minimum level of confidence – you wouldn't like to be known for your real name by everyone.

You can publish books using your real name, but those books must represent you and be truly professional. If you want to publish books under your real name, you should also create a page on Amazon's Author Central Page – I will cover this next.

Chapter 10: Author Central Page

Author Central is a tool offered by Amazon that will help you reach more readers – your customers who liked you will start following you and you will increase your sales potential.

You can tweet, read customers' comments, and track your Author Ranking – every author who has a page on Author Central is ranked individually, just like the books are, and the rank is updated every day.

You can write your biography there, and by doing this, you will provide trust to your potential readers, they will now who they are buying from.

To set up an Author Central page, you will have to go to www.authorcentral.amazon.com

Chapter 11: Using Box Sets

Box Set = Bundle = 2in1 Books, 3in1 Books, X in 1 Books, etc. These are multiple books in one with a lower price.

If you have similar books, books on the same topic, a series of books, or just some books that just go well together, by using a bundle, you will attract more readers. From 2 books, for example, you will have the 2 books individually and the Bundle that is practically from the same 2 books. In other words, you create 3 books out of 2 and you will generate additional income from it.

People will be encouraged to borrow Bundles as you offer them a larger amount of information for a lower price.

How do you price your Bundles?

If you have 2 books at $2.99, for example, so they are $5.98 in total for both, you can sell the 2in1 Bundle for $3.99 (-30%), you will surely have sales and borrows at least half of what you are already earning for the other 2 books individually.

Imagine you have a series of 10 books. You can make 2in1, 3in1, 5in1 or even 10in1. What does it cost you? An hour to edit a Book Cover or $ 5 to create a new one? You will surely generate income by doing this, it's a good marketing strategy – you use the resources that you already have.

Conclusion

Thank you once again for downloading and reading this book. I truly hope that you have gained the knowledge and value I have put into this book, the illustrations and images are screenshots from my account that I openly shared with you here. I am sure that you are now able to start your own Kindle business by keeping the steps, tips, and tricks I have written here in mind.

I honestly request a review from you, as it helps me a lot to improve my future books.

Kindest Regards,

Frank